The Colors
of
Relationships

*Using the insights of
Colors to strengthen
the relationship with
your partner*

George J. Boelcke, CCP

Also by George Boelcke:

- Colorful Personalities: Discover Your Personality Type Through the Power of Colors
- Colorful Personalities: Audio CD
- The Colors of Leadership and Management
- The Colors of Sales and Customers
- The Colors of Parent and Child Dynamics
- Colors Tools for Christians
- Colors At Work
- Money Tools & Rules: Borrow Smarter, pay less, and reach your debt freedom (Canadian edition)
- Fighting Back! How to take back financial control, restore your credit and reach your debt freedom (US edition)

To Contact the Author:

George Boelcke facilitates seminars throughout North America for companies and organizations ranging from Fortune 500 firms to small businesses, church groups, relationship seminars, conventions and schools. George can be contacted:

By e-mail: george@vantageseminars.com
Via web-site: www.vantageseminars.com

Library and Archives Canada Cataloguing in Publication

Boelcke, George J., 1959–
      The colors of relationships : using the insights of colors to strengthen the relationship with your partner / George J. Boelcke.

Includes index.
ISBN 978-0-9736668-7-8

      1. Interpersonal relations. 2. Color—Psychological aspects.
      I. Title.

HQ801.B63 2006   158.2   C2006-902238-0.

Design assistance: David Macpherson
Layout & typeset by: Ingénieuse Productions, Edmonton, AB
Printed and Bound in the United States of America

Contents

*"I see your true colors shining through
and that's why I love you.
So don't be afraid to let them show –
your true colors— a beautiful you."*
Phil Collins

There are few things in life better than a successful and happy relationship. It is almost like a little piece of heaven here on earth. Conversely, a dysfunctional relationship with problems, a lack of meaningful communication, or truly understanding each other is exactly the opposite. And the ramifications leak into all other areas of our life, affecting us at work and our overall mood and mindset.

Understanding Colors has many powerful values to strengthen every relationship and almost create a new dimension for them. It is somewhat like getting a new set of glasses through which to view your partner, their strengths, habits, core values, and motivators. But even with a new set of glasses and a different insight, it is still up to you to choose honoring your partner in the language of their Colors. While this book deals with the relationships of couples, many of the tools apply equally effectively to all other people in your life. After all, Webster's defines a relationship as a state of being mutually interested, or involved. And to relate is simply to favorably connect with someone.

A large number of the skills we use in our relationship we first learned from observing our parents. We emulate many of the things that worked in their life. But it is often confusing when those tools do not work. After all, our partner can be very different from our parents, in their Colors, and many other ways.

The first time someone is sick, what a shock when an Orange partner does not spends their entire day nursing them back to health. They'll check in on you, give you a few minutes of sympathy, but they still need to be out doing stuff and having fun.

Perhaps it is a serious operation needed by a high Green. Which will turn to doing extensive research before ever trusting the doctor. Their need for Green alone-time will increase and can develop a single-minded focus on understanding, researching, and generally dealing with this on their own. How devastating to a high Blue partner who wants to feel and share the emotions and pain. In their view, a serious illness is the time to get closer, to share and support each other. Instead, the Green partner is spending a lot of time on various websites researching and pulling off as much information as possible.

For many, it is refreshing to have a partner who really gets things done, plans, and executes— and actually sticks to their schedule. However, it won't be long before these Gold traits can perhaps run against their partner's need to accommodate people, or have fun and stay flexible on a decision. At that point it is a rude awakening when there turns out to be almost no on-off switch to accommodate their partner.

Without the tools and understanding of Colors, at some early point, in some minor ways, it can become a mindset that one partner is right and the other is wrong instead of just different.

*One of your biggest strengths
is acknowledging your shortcomings.*

It's Not About Changing Them

"I love you just the way you are."
Billy Joel

One of the alternatives that many couples try, (or are practicing already) is attempting to change their partner— or at least some of their personality. The bad news is that it won't last. Take an elastic band and pull it apart with both hands. Now hold it there— forever. OK, how long can you hold it? If you let go, the elastic will return right back to its original shape— or it will snap. That is the same as focusing on changing your partner. They'll walk, be resentful, or at best make some temporary small change. But nothing that has a lasting impact. Maybe it creates temporary change— at worst it creates a scar and resentment.

Understanding Colors will not give you any tips or tricks to change your partner. Having a different outlook or interpretation of someone's behavior is always up to you. To have some different results— you have to do some different things. It is not about forcing change, but about embracing your diverse strengths and loving your partner for who they really are. In other words, to look for the value in them and to choose to focus on their unique, special gifts, talents and contributions to your relationship. To be aware of your Colors, and those of your partner, creates powerful tools in your relationship.

So stop thinking, wondering, hoping, wishing, or even wanting to make them change. You can control, and are accountable, only for your own actions. You cannot change many things in life, just like you cannot change your partner— but you can control every reaction you have, and every step you take to fight it, or choose to look for the value in it.

7

In the Beginning ...

Many singles wouldn't want to date someone who wasn't good looking, perhaps too tall, too short, not the right hair color or perhaps not rich enough, or maybe the wrong clothes or the fact that their _____ is too _____. But chances are, they are not reading this in any event. For many singles it is an overriding drive to find someone who is physically attractive and looks great— who is worthy of pursuit.

Are those the important factors to look for when you need your partner to help you through a tragedy? Is that the overriding factor when you're celebrating a huge milestone of your daughter or son? Or when you need someone to trust you unconditionally? Are those the factors which form your decisions? Is it looking good or being good that matters in the relationship? Those aren't ever things to look for with friendships— yet in today's society they're important when it comes to picking a life partner?

In the book, *Colorful Personalities*, the chapter on relationships discusses how different Colors first tend to start dating, and how opposites attract. Gold will generally become friends first, although it is very hard to get into their inner circle of friends. They value traditional dating methods and more formal courtship, while building trust and often working their way into someone's heart with their strong desire to be helpful through frequently doing many acts of service.

Blue connects with people through their heart. While they will not readily be able to explain it, their strong sense of intuition will let them see the real person inside. It is also a Color that looks for the good in everyone, always finding a positive thing to say, or many ways of looking at any issue or behavior.

Green seeks to make an intellectual connection first and foremost. Their logical mind understands that a partner should be someone that can also challenge them, help them grow, and share their drive and desire to learn, explore, question and remain independent.

Orange is certainly the most pro-active group when it comes to dating. They will be the largest group of women who actually ask men out. What's the point sitting back instead of going after what they want? Dating for them also becomes more of a speed issue. They will readily see their new friend many days in a row, and feel they know the person extremely well after only a short period of time. They'll lay their cards on the table and tend to share everything, instead of being careful just to put their best foot forward. To them, dating me makes you one of the luckiest people around, so enjoy it. If not, I'll move on— no big deal.

Your life isn't measured by what you do
and people don't experience you as you are,
but only as they see you.

When you are first dating, you look for and bring out the best in each other. All dating is playful, fun, and spontaneous. You stay flexible to the needs and desires of your partner and are more than willing to go along with ideas and plans. At that time, there is seldom an issue of not wanting to expand your horizons, stretch your comfort zone and try new things. You're flexible and fun! After all, you're pretty much selling yourself aren't you?

Then at some point, you get back to your routine— the real life of life. Of the routines, daily stuff, challenges, obstacles, and all those real things. If the fun leaves your relationship, can trouble be far behind? This can be many ways for different Colors. Is it getting back to being skeptical? Back to more concerned and worried than fun? More routine than going with the flow? Perhaps more of ignoring each other, taking the other person for granted, or just not connecting with the *real* other person any more?

You could easily have seen some of your challenges coming. Just remember back to what the relationship was like in the first six months. Go back— have fun again and stop letting the realities of life consume your relationship. After all, isn't it more important than all that other stuff? Make a commitment to go back to the beginning, in a way. Remember back to the first month and have a first date again, it's worth it to re-connect in real and meaningful ways.

Whether it's pizza or Paris, it's not where you go – it's who you go with.

Two great individuals should naturally make a perfect couple. Unfortunately, it doesn't work that way. In the first serious disagreement, each Colors' unique strengths will start to come to the surface in now wanting to have them adopted as standard operating procedure. But in those early battles, one partner learns that their way of doing something has really been poor, or wrong, for all those years of being single. Without intending to, one partner or the other, depending on each situation, is made to feel dumb, disorganized, too talkative, not serious enough, or just plain wrong. Because if opposites attract, it is generally after the first few months that each person discovers there is another side to their partner which can cause challenges and irritations, and it is frequently their social styles where it becomes an issue.

In any relationship, major challenges draw both partners together. But it is the annoying minor things that can pull them apart. Putting away the dishes, not finishing projects, not paying the bills on time or not even knowing there is a certain way the toothpaste "has" to be squeezed can all be challenges.

Successful relationships are based on a foundation of friendship that continues to work toward meeting each other's needs in a framework of honesty and open communication. You don't need to wait for your partner to make changes in the relationship— it doesn't take the other person to start— it just takes you! After all... garbage in— garbage out.

So start with yourself: Positive changes in— better results out. And for most people, it just means a different view of their partner by having a deeper understanding of their unique Colors.

First, focus and understand your own response to any situation instead of attempting to change your partner.

There are some specific things with which each Color might require help and support. In the next chapter are many commonly seen issues for each different Color combination, plus two further points that may apply just for you or perhaps your partner. These may be some of your stresses or could simply be conflicts through your introvert or extrovert personality type.

A powerful tool to growing your relationship is to openly and honestly communicate with your partner. After all, relationships aren't 50-50— that is just the divorce rate. It is always 100-100. In the next few days, without the television, kids, or interruptions, spend a few minutes with each other and circle your important conflicts or stresses from the next section. Go through these with your partner and give him or her an example of the last time this issue caused stress or conflict. If you're both prepared to look at each other's Colors in a loving and open way, to do more of what works in your relationship, you'd be amazed at the results. Always remember that your partner is not doing any ot these things to annoy you, but only because he or she doesn't know any different.

Some Common Gold Relationship Stresses

- Changing my routine
- Changing your mind after we agreed
- Clutter & anything unorganized
- Exceptions to the rules
- Forgetting some details
- Getting sidetracked
- Having to wing it or not having a plan
- Inconsistency
- Indecision
- Interruptions
- Lack of clear direction
- Last minute change of plans
- Losing control
- Making plans for me
- No cooperation or help with: _____
- Not enough time
- Not getting something totally finished and done
- Promises not kept
- Questioning me
- Reactive and scrambling
- Running late
- Setting my priorities
- Stuck with too much responsibility
- Telling me to just leave it until tomorrow
- Too many things undone
- Waiting for you
- When it's not done right
- _____
- _____
- _____

Some Common Blue Relationship Stresses

- Arguments or conflict
- Being taken advantage of
- Being yelled at
- Challenging or discounting my intuition
- Criticism & harsh tone of voice
- Deadlines
- Feeling I haven't done enough
- Feelings hurt easily when you: _____
- Finding the time to see friends & volunteer
- Frustrated by inflexibility
- Judgmental comments about others
- Lack of empathy
- Lack of humor & being too serious
- Lingering conflict & disharmony
- Making fun of me
- Missing romance, hugs & holding hands
- No help in saying no or setting boundaries
- Not being taken seriously when I'm emotional
- Not getting enough support
- Not having time for myself
- Paperwork or housework as a priority
- Telling me I'm overreacting
- The silent treatment
- Wanting to please everyone
- When you don't call just to say hi
- When you don't share from your heart
- Worrying about others' problems
- _____
- _____
- _____

Some Common Orange Relationship Stresses

- A *'you have to'* attitude or approach
- Being on the sidelines
- Boredom & lack of action
- Conformity
- Cutting off my need to talk it through
- Feelings hurt when I'm not politically correct
- Getting asked too many questions
- Having to be on time
- Having to finish everything
- Holding me to all my promises or commitments
- Lack of choices and options
- Lingering conflict or argument
- Not enough challenges
- Not enough spending money
- Not supporting or finding the positives in my ideas
- Organizing or moving my stuff around
- Paperwork & paying bills
- Restricting my freedom when you: _____
- Rigid plans when something better comes up
- Routines and sameness
- Sitting still and doing nothing
- Spending time alone
- Structure & rules
- Stuck inside
- Talking about stuff from the past
- Too many rules
- Too much stuff planned out or piled on
- Whining, complaining and worrying
- _____
- _____
- _____

Some Common Green Relationship Stresses

- Artificial deadlines
- Emotional outbursts
- Forgetting something
- Getting bad or incorrect information
- Having to come along to every social function
- Incompetence – self & others
- Inefficiencies
- Insufficient information
- Interruptions when I: _____
- Know I'm right & you question it
- Not enough alone time
- No challenges/too much repetition & routines
- Noise
- Not enough time to read or be on the computer
- Not knowing or understanding
- Not listening when I'm teaching you something
- Questioning my decision or reasoning
- Quick decisions to important questions
- Relying on other's thought process
- Rules & restrictions that don't make sense
- Some of your friends & relatives
- Talks without a point
- Telling me I don't look happy or I should smile
- Too many routines
- What TV channel to watch
- When you push me for a decision or answer
- Worrying about forgetting something
- _____
- _____
- _____

Things We Need From Each Other

Gold Needs Help from Blue to:

- promote them
- help them dream bigger
- stay more positive
- soften their directness
- not just look at the practical side of things
- expand their circle of friends
- relax and live for the moment
- share the load of their to-do list
- put people over tasks

Specifically, I need your high Blue strengths and talents to help me with:

- _____
- _____

Blue Needs Help from Gold to:

- be more direct
- have structure
- not take comments personally at times
- plan, organize & execute
- help implement their big ideas and dreams
- feel safe & cared for unconditionally
- not make them feel guilty
- reach closure and decisions
- face negative issues and resolve conflict directly

Specifically, I need your high Gold strengths and talents to help me with:

- _____
- _____

Gold Needs Help from Green to:

- stay calm under stress & pressure
- focus on quality over quantity
- set limits and say no
- expand their lateral thinking skills
- embrace growth and change
- grow beyond today tasks & to-do lists
- look at the big picture first
- worry less often about fewer issues
- not over-organize their life

Specifically, I need your high Green strengths and talents to help me with:

- _____
- _____

Green Needs Help from Gold to:

- handle the details, mundane & daily tasks
- get closure and focus on completion
- set deadlines and adhere to schedules
- differentiate between getting it done vs. perfect
- remember birthdays, anniversaries & social occasions
- take care of social niceties, thank you cards, etc.
- focus their drive for improvements & progress
- get organized and stay on task

Specifically, I need your high Gold strengths and talents to help me with:
- _____
- _____

Gold Needs Help from Orange to:

- wing it sometimes and not over-plan
- not take many things so serious
- expand their people skills
- learn their positive demeanor
- grow their no fear, don't worry & can-do disposition
- be more of a risk-taker at times
- stay flexible, avoid too many rules & time issues
- help grow their creativity and optimism
- not measure things by money & ease up on budget

Specifically, I need your high Orange strengths and talents to help me with:

- _____

- _____

Orange Needs Help from Gold to:

- remember getting the tasks done
- set priorities & keep their word
- gain focus, direction and details
- help with paperwork, organization & savings
- pick the times to be spontaneous
- implement their ideas with details
- channel their endless energies
- learn some of their drive for traditions
- find the value in planning things in advance

Specifically, I need your high Gold strengths and talents to help me with:

- _____

- _____

Green Needs Help from Orange to:

- be flexible and sometimes just do it
- promote simplicity
- do their shopping, plus fashion & style input
- emulate some of their spontaneity at times
- expand their social skills
- soften their skeptical demeanor

- talk more without filtering their thoughts
- make them laugh
- be more receptive to changing tracks or decisions

Specifically, I need your high Orange strengths and talents to help me with:
- _____
- _____

Orange Needs Help from Green to:

- honestly share their hurts and pain
- value having all the information before acting
- give them new challenges & avoid boredom
- watch their impulse actions & purchases
- help them focus and set priorities
- make their ideas and creativity practical & doable
- slow down more often
- sometimes think things through before acting or talking

Specifically, I need your high Green strengths and talents to help me with:
- _____
- _____

Green Needs Help from Blue to:

- remember the people effect & aspects
- soften their words & sarcasm
- expand their social skills
- soften their need for credibility in everything and everyone
- grow their interactive communication tools
- recognize when people come first
- understand the difference between listening and fixing
- discuss & share feelings openly
- limit their Green (alone) time to reasonable amounts

Specifically, I need your high Blue strengths and talents to help me with:
- _____
- _____

Blue Needs Help from Green to:

- bring problems back to real size
- see when logic can come ahead of feelings
- not take things personally
- set boundaries & look after themselves
- promote, encourage and make practical their big dreams and goals
- be aware of their sensitivity at times
- verbalize their own wishes more often
- communicate more directly
- face negative issues head-on

Specifically, I need your high Green strengths and talents to help me with:

* _____

* _____

Orange Needs Help from Blue to:

• soften their direct and blunt approach

• deepen relationships

• teach them sensitivity

• slow down and enjoy the moment

• value time together instead of competition

• remember birthdays & anniversaries

• reduce their impatience level

• share their 'helping others first' approach

• be cognizant of hurt feelings

Specifically, I need your high Blue strengths and talents to help me with:

* _____

* _____

Blue Needs Help from Orange to:

• bring their fears & worries to realistic size

• shorten up their conversations at times

• forgive & forget more often

• stand up for them & sometimes be the bad guy and say 'no' on their behalf

- help them set boundaries and take care of themselves
- gain the energies to make their dreams come true
- avoid frequent "what did I do wrong" feelings
- be more direct & straight forward
- get over things quicker

Specifically, I need your high Orange strengths and talents to help me with:
- _____
- _____

Perhaps you can also consider, or share with your partner, the impact of your Colors with respect to the following:

- What do you choose to give your partner or withhold from them that they need?

- I want more...

- I can give you more...

- My partner needs more...

- I can be more flexible with...

- Truthfully, the core strength of my Color that I've been wanting to 'teach' my partner is...

*"The anal-retentive side of you
is not gonna help you get girls."*
(Response to enforcing policies)
CJ Cregg to Charlie: The West Wing

Your Gold Partner

- Gold values being in control of their agenda and their world. Honor this strength, but keep them mindful when it starts to leak out into wanting to teach others these same skills.

- Challenge them to pick the times when their sense of worry and planning are important, but find the off switch when it is unnecessary and not helpful.

- They are direct, in an effort to get things done efficiently and off their list.

- Stay aware of their stress to get it done and resolved. For example, Gold thinks Green agrees just because they don't say anything. Yet Green really wanted time to decide—then discuss it next week.

- Gold (and Green) can withdraw. Show a small amount of affection in their love language, and Color, and watch the relationship blossom in a couple of days.

- Most things are right or wrong, black or white. When their partner does not fit into these categories on certain issues it can become stressful. Teach them to look at a variety of ways.

- Appreciate the value of their organizational strengths. There are definite ways a kitchen is organized or things are put away. Yes, they would rather be happy instead of right.

But their actions will often betray that. In a loving way, remind them of the importance of staying flexible without giving up their core values. These strengths create structure, safety and security for Gold. While it is always in a caring way, they do want others to learn and adapt some of these traits. Unless you're high Gold, you probably don't even know that there's a certain way to eat grapes, for instance. It should really be done by taking off one stem at a time. It keeps the bowl organized and the rest of them looking neat. Definitely not just grabbing some from everywhere and having half eaten stems sticking out all over the place.

• Challenge them to have an Orange day once in a while, or to not wear their watch on the weekend. It is possible. Not to change them, but to grow and stretch their horizon and not to have all their play time planned out.

• Agree to times when their to-do list goes away to have fun and relax. In the meantime, honor them with the time to get as many things done and off the list as possible.

"You know how hard it is for us Golds to change. But I promise to at least make sure that my strengths don't have to be shared by everybody and to first remember my husband's strength instead of getting critical."
High Gold from a thank-you note.

The Value of Traditions

Keeping traditions alive is the specialty of our Gold friends. In an article by Bishop Michael Pryse in the *Lutheran Magazine*, Bishop Pryse argues that contemporary is not always superior to the traditional. While new insights, change and growth are always important and welcome, traditions allow us to stay in touch with a broader understanding which very much shapes who we are and preserves our roots and rich history. Or as G.K. Chesterton explained it: "Tradition means giving votes to our ancestors. " In fact, we get input into the next generations, as our grandparents get a small say into what we do today. A vote and input – not a veto – into some of the traditions, cultures and ways we do things today. "We've always done it that way", is often an excuse or defense, but shouldn't be confused with allowing and helping Golds to keep many traditions alive.

Always remember the powerful strengths of your Gold partner:

... accurate confident traditional sincere loyal conservative decisive prompt self-confident thorough supportive caring fair honest organized leaders punctual conforming practical consistent thoughtful stable empathetic efficient in control focused responsible giving helpful reliable conscientious reasonable savers structured take-charge respected traditional accomplishment... and so many more.

Your Blue partner is always willing to take their time to spare and turn it into time to share.

• While they won't verbalize it, there can be feelings that a relationship is too good to be true, the feeling of perhaps not being deserving.

• Like the rest of their life, Blue can often put their own wishes and desires aside for the sake of their partner. After all, standing up for themselves is hard at the best of times. Make them feel totally safe that any sign of pursuing their desires and dreams will not affect the relationship. They want to belong, be liked and loved so it is a little scary to stand up for their needs.

• A relationship with a high Blue puts an onus on their partner to create ways through actions, words, physical touch and reassurance to enable them to feel this unconditional love and safety.

• Blue can use feelings and tears as a weapon to create compassion. It can be an indirect way of looking out for themselves, as others will find them so warm and caring that they will give in. Help them be direct and assist them in standing up for themselves.

• Value their special strength of being a people Color and consistent fighter for the underdog.

• Recognize their strength of forming social bonds, remembering birthdays and always doing the little and special things to connect with others from the heart.

- Understand their feelings of forgiving but seldom forgetting. They will be the judge of whether your apology is genuine and whether it will be accepted.

- Assure they have their need for self-esteem builders met. Often that includes encouraging and supporting them to become involved with volunteer groups outside the home.

- Blue will often swallow hard, put on their happy face, stay positive, and not let others see they've been hurt. One day it will all come out after being bottled up so long. Be mindful of their need to talk things through and not to be fixed in order to bring healing to them. After all, feelings buried alive never die.

- Be aware of their hurt feelings when they keep giving and doing and it isn't reciprocated. Help them to know that there is only so much energy to go around and to use it where it is appreciated or really needed. There is nothing selfish about looking after themselves first so they have the energy to be of value to others.

"I know he loves me, but...alright I promise to just practice asking for what I want a little bit. I know it'll be ok but it's really hard. He's great, I don't want him to feel like I'm turning selfish..."
High Blue lady after a seminar.

The Power of Intuition

Michael Touhey testified before the 9/11 commission. On September 11th, 2001, Michael was on the early shift at the US Airways ticket counter in Maine. Less than two hours into his shift, he ticketed two men on their way to Boston. Immediately, Michael's intuition told him "if anyone looked like terrorists, it's these two." Yet he testified that he immediately felt bad for having thought something so terrible about these two. Besides, it was in the pre 9/11 environment. As the day unfolded, it turned out that these were two of the terrorists who hijacked one of the flights departing out of Boston.

Michael shared that he spent a lot of time crying and feeling regrets and pain over what he didn't do or say – and likely still feels the pain to this day. It was never his responsibility until post 9/11 measures were implemented. Yet so many times high Blues can face not only their own question of whether to follow their intuition or not – but also whether to share their insights with anyone.

Always remember the powerful strengths of your Blue partner:

... friendly generous trustworthy warm kind-hearted intuitive democratic creative loving sincere romantic peace-makers tactful honest caring sensitive loyal patient forgiving optimistic feelings compassionate spiritual eye contact genuine laughter great listeners huggers easy-going inclusive humor flexible dreamers polite ... and so many more.

*"If my heart could do the thinking
would my brain begin to feel?"*
Van Morrison

- One of the harder lessons to learn is that high Greens are very easy going— to a point. Somewhere you will find the trigger where a certain issue or way of doing things really matters to them. At that point, they will definitely dig their heals in and want to get their way— and it won't be open for discussion.

- Don't trigger the Green sense of annoyance by questioning their intelligence.

- Ask neutral questions of '*what about...*' instead of '*have you thought about this...*' — of course they have.

- Be mindful that they are giving you (better) information instead of feeling that you are being criticized.

- Going away to think is NOT something you did wrong— it is an important part of their life— always.

- If you're pushing for an instant answer, it may often be 'no.' Do you want the right answer or quick answer?

- Teach them the importance of open communications. If you are high Blue, you need to call just to say hello. Green (and Gold) will generally only call to pass on information or confirm things. They are not Colors to call for 'no reason,' as they can view it.

- Discussing feelings is harder for high Greens than other Colors. Teach them it is OK and important to you and the relationship. Or in the words of the Lone Star song: *"Show her what you're feeling, tell her you're believing, even though it's hard to say."*

"My wife is Blue, I've learned to call her once a day for no reason. Well, I'm running about 60%. Truthfully, it drives me nuts. I have things to think about, stuff to do and it cuts into my Green time. But it makes her happy and I realize it's very important to her."
E-mail from a Green/Gold

- Green has the view that facts stand until better information comes along. That will not work in building stronger relationships, especially if they are with the people Colors of Orange and Blue. Both of them need verbal affirmations, assurance, attention and communication.

Many Greens have learned this and adapted their communication style to honor their partner. An easy question is always when a Green is asked how often they tell their Blue partner (opposites attract, remember?) "I love you" or whether they've adapted to willingly hold hands in public?

Always remember the powerful strengths of your Green partner:

...analytical logical knowledge credibility teaching independent theoretical rational learning honest innovative curious informative skeptical visionaries well-read inquisitive future-oriented self-confident easy-going focused direct non-fiction ingenuity questioning calm-cool-collected problem-solving informed intelligent self-directed creative big picture to the point... and so many more.

The "F" Word

For most high Greens, the "F" word is feelings, but first things first. Greens feel, care and hurt just as deeply as any other Colors. Where they differ is in their way of expressing it— NOT in the way they feel it. Any perception that they don't, simply comes out of the judgments of your Colors. High Greens also don't fight or have emotional outbursts very often. To them, it would just be illogical. But they will be prepared to discuss the issues all day long.

Even when it comes to thinking about their own emotional reactions, they often question themselves as to whether they're feeling that or thinking that, whether it's logical or real. In their own hurts and pain, almost all Greens will want to have 'cave time' to deal with their issues. They would far prefer to lock themselves away and think it through rather than spending time with others in talking through their feelings.

Your Green Partner

"I'm opinionated, I'm a Scorpio and a red-head. I'll tell you what I'm thinking— don't you worry."
TNN: Blind Date participant

• Having an Orange tell you what's on their mind is seldom an issue. If nothing else, they'll let you have it— direct, now, and without mincing words.

• Your Orange partner can show impatience through interrupting and finishing your sentences unless they focus on slowing down for a while— or for a reason.

• They do like attention and can be loud, very outgoing and boisterous— definitely the life of a party. Besides, in their head there is a party all the time. You won't change them, but be honest in telling them that there are times when you need the volume control turned down, and other times when you are actually quite envious and proud.

• Be aware of their challenge to stop kidding around and being honest. It is also a stress for them when others don't realize they are being serious.

• Orange uses their humor to blow over and cover their hurts. Make it safe and give them the time to share honestly what their fears, concerns and pains really are. Yes, they have them, but not many people will ever get to see or hear it.

• They look for a positive demeanor and can-do attitude and pick up lots of non-verbal clues. It does come with potential dangers.

The frequent demeanor of Gold is one of concern, while Greens tend to be skeptical, or at least quiet, and much more introvert. That is a challenge for the Orange upbeat, high-energy outlook on life.

- Be aware that Orange can vote with their feet. They want to get away from many situations where they start feeling boxed in, dominated or controlled. Really hear them when Orange starts expressing ways they are feeling in these situations. That often-present feeling that there's something better out there and a frequent drive to find it. It may sound cruel, but it is one of the reasons Orange will likely choose a common-law relationship instead of being *officially* committed to a relationship.

- When they mess up your stuff or get playful, an Orange is not doing it to annoy you. It's their playful way to pull you out of your comfort zone, to relax, have fun and play and not take many things so seriously.

- Get them to buy into following important rules. Too many and for no *'good'* reason won't work, so share honestly which ones are important to you. With valid reasons and their specific agreement, they will understand the importance and honor your needs.

"OK, now it makes sense. He's Gold and this explains it. I promise not to make him totally Orange and let him do all that planning which gives me a headache. But I'm gonna keep working on getting him out of his comfort zone. I can do it— I can do anything. Besides, he enjoyed it when we started going out."
Paraphrased from an Orange call.

Always remember the powerful strengths of your Orange partner:

... action optimistic dynamic flexible vocal humor fun impulsive spontaneous skillful direct social generous freedom creative artistic multi-taskers negotiators fast-paced entertaining loyal caring risk-takers adventurous active people-magnet open-minded great with tools attention-getting winging it never bored low stress just do it... and so many more

Getting Mad

Disagreements do happen in any relationship. However the important factor is how they are resolved when frustration or hurt feelings turn to anger. Anger is aroused by sense of injustice, injury, or insult. It is a natural human expression, a part of us all, and covers a wide range of moral outrage, annoyance, or minor stuff. Often it is the blowing over of frustrations. It may be at others, sometimes at ourselves, or often involving circumstances which are totally out of our control.

The first thing to do is to be honest with yourself. Yes, it is OK to get angry. It is just not acceptable to lash out, or to let your frustrations out in that manner. It is not an excuse to be hurtful in words or actions.

It does help to put physical distance between you and the source of the anger, if possible. Walk away, take a time-out, or at least take a deep breath and count to 50. Until then, you are no good to anyone. Anything other than a time-out with yourself most often exasperates the situations instead of resolving the problem. Feelings buried alive never die and suppressed anger often leads to depression. Remove— reflect— resolve will always be three valuable steps in this situation.

It is important to get to the real source of the anger. Often it is the basic frustrations of our Colors that play a big part. It is important to acknowledge honestly what the reasons are. Whether they are just perceptions of situations or real frustrations over others' behaviors, or brought on by the natural stresses of our Colors, you will always have to face it to replace it.

When a situation involves others, letting the problem fester creates a wedge between ourselves and others. It needs to be dealt with before becoming all consuming. Let forgiveness work— and share it. Almost all of us know how to lash out, fight back and to hurt each other. We know what we always do when we're angry, and just what buttons to press when we want to get even. Commit to taking the same intuitions and use the understanding of your partner's Colors to nurture, support, build each other up, and make each other happy in the language of our Colors.

Blue and Orange can tell by your face if something's wrong. They are more instinctive, and better at reading people. With Golds and Greens you have to tell them.

What's So Funny?

How is your sense of humor? No kidding— this is serious. A sense of humor is one of the easiest stress relievers and stress prevention tools in life. It is also one of the most important factors we look for in our relationships. It reduces grief and grants relief. Study after study shows that it is one of the top three things each Color looks for in their partner.

After all, whether our general demeanor is skeptical, concerned or optimistic, we all value others that are positive and don't take themselves too seriously. We may not be able to emulate it all the time, but we are secretly a little envious more often than not. Perhaps not to the stage of ever saying 'Don't worry— be happy' but to view most things with a healthy sense of humor will always keep stressful situations in check and limited to their real size. It is certainly one of the most important things all of our Orange friends live daily and can teach others so well.

How Do You Fight?

"I'd rather go through any pain love puts us through than to spend one day without you by my side."
Barbara Streisand & Vince Gill

For each Color group, there are some common ways they tend to deal with conflict. Is it an all out battle where winning is the most important factor? Winning at all cost is a trait that can be very valuable. Just not when it comes to arguments. Do you tend to walk away? Not just to cool off for a couple of minutes— but for hours or days on end? Ignoring the situation will not make it go away. In fact, to take that approach with a high Blue partner deepens the wounds and will always hurt much more than whatever the original argument was about— always.

Perhaps it is to yell and scream for a few minutes, only to quickly realize that the situation is getting out of hand. At that point, do you assume it is all over and move on? Has anything been resolved unless you discuss it again when cooler heads prevail? If not, isn't it a given that the same situation will arise again and again? Well, the definition of insanity is doing the same thing over and over and somehow expecting different results. It won't happen.

Is it possible for you to find a common Color to resolve your arguments in? No, not in the heat of the battle. At that point, few people are calm enough to want anything but to defend themselves— or to go on the offensive. But it is very helpful to find a common Color to handle these situations in. For the four groups, that could involve:

- Let's discuss it right now, be honest and blunt, tell me what you're feeling and thinking and we'll get this resolved quickly, move on and forget about it.

- We'll do a list of the two or three things we want to discuss. Then we will commit to focus on one thing at a time, stay on the subject, resolve it, and be able to cross it off our to-do list.

- First we will take some alone time to cool down and think about it, each on our own. When we discuss it, we will not raise our voices, won't over-talk it, or get emotional about the subject. We will stay calm and cool and talk logically to find the best solution we can brainstorm between us and agree to. When some better solution presents itself in the future, we will re-visit it at that point to grow into a better solution.

- There will never be a question that the foundation of our relationship is strong. Our love for each other will not make this disagreement very important in the big picture of our partnership. We will sit together holding hands, and by our physical touch will make it almost impossible to stay hostile while we talk. We will immediately connect in caring ways that make our fight seem so much smaller. We will not lash out at each other or say hurtful things, but will share our feelings honestly and from the heart. Afterwards, we will both apologize. It never matters who won or who was right, but it matters that we forgive and forget and that we grow stronger in our relationship, understanding and love for each other.

Last but not least, it is valuable to remember that a sure-fire way to scare many men (only because they tend to be the much larger group of Gold and Green) by saying *'we need to talk.'* Often, they are hearing it as the equivalent of *'you're fired'* from their boss. Or it can mean "I have to talk and you have to sit there and listen." Should that be the case, change the melody, but not the song. In the special ways of your Color, approach getting to the talking stage in different ways without changing what you wish to discuss. But always be mindful of the primary Color of your partner and their ways of communicating.

Don't Make Meaningful Conversations an Event

Let it happen, don't make it happen.

Let's face it, meaningful conversations that involve sharing dreams and goals are an important part of getting closer with your partner. They grow your intimacy and bonds. Unfortunately, they are also not very safe to discuss, which is why many people stick to fact talk, weather talk, their day at work, and the kids instead. Feelings can't be hurt and you will never be vulnerable when conversations are restricted to those areas. It is very sad— but very true. Or perhaps it is just wanting to talk about situations and issues before they become a big problem and a larger fight or disagreement results.

The time to talk has to be mutual and not driven by one partner's agenda. The consequence to pushing ahead without getting the commitment that now is the time, is a pretty sure-fire recipe for trouble and will often create a bad outcome or no resolution. To get past that point, there are some common Color issues that often should be considered:

Green needs to open up and share from the heart without filtering their thoughts. To understand that their partner is the one person they can trust unconditionally and share their hurts and feelings with, no matter what. Orange needs to put all other things aside and focus solely on their partner's needs for a while. To press the mental pause button on their sense of humor and to listen more and talk less.

Blue needs to feel and know that honesty, openness, and directness will not affect the relationship, no matter what they say. That it is OK to state their needs and ask for what they want. Gold needs to put their natural defensive mechanism aside. To stay out of their judgment and not be concerned with filtering the discussion through a scale of what they did wrong. After all, it is about sharing, caring and growing, not a right or wrong discussion.

Hearing vs. Understanding

"He Said— She Heard."
Sean Morley song title

Yes, there is a big difference between hearing and understanding. We keep saying we understand, but do we really? Marriage counselors often say that the number one tool for success in a relationship is understanding each other. We think we do, but for sure we can hear the other person out, and that is often a great start. Understanding necessitates knowing the mindset and feelings of the other person. For the four different Color groups, that would be quite a stretch indeed, to actually understand their mindset.

It is certain that when you are not listening you are not bringing healing when your partner is speaking. How much listening are you doing if you start getting your reply ready half way through their sharing? Or if you are already starting to build your case for the defense, and filtering their comments through the view of your Color? In addition to the last section, there are two very frequently seen examples of this:

As Gold is the largest group in the country, the first one involves this Color. Anyone high Blue communicates quite often in an indirect manner. The words can be *'we should'* instead of a direct *'please do'* or *'would you?'* But most high

Golds immediately hear that they should take this on and add it to their to-do list. It is their mindset of having to do it, if it needs to be done. That was not what the high Blue person was saying but, way more times than not, what the Gold person is hearing.

Hearing versus understanding also involves high Greens in many situations. They love teaching and having others learn what they discover or know. Comments or feedback from a high Green are often judged as criticism. Nothing could be further from the truth. Almost all high Greens will gladly tell you that it is not criticism. From work to relationships, they are giving you information. Better information than you are working with, in their view. There is a big difference between sharing information and criticism. But once again, the filter of our Color, or a lack of understanding your partner's Color, makes it quite a different mindset.

Communication isn't just the talking part.

How Others Make It Work

It is always difficult to look at the relationships of others and attempt to figure out how those people can possibly make it work. After all, every marriage, combination of Colors in a relationship, and different personality types is very unique, different and difficult to judge as an outsider.

An easy couple to consider is certainly Bill and Hillary Clinton. Rumors abounded that these two were only staying together as a political power couple. Outsiders guessed that they were using each other, would divorce as soon as Clinton left the White House, as soon as Hillary was elected to the Senate or many other rumors and speculations, all of which have so far proven false. After all, most people can only compare the lives of others through their own belief system and through the glasses and values of their unique Colors. It becomes more of an "I would or wouldn't" view, rather than attempting to understand the unique dynamics, strengths and values of the actual couple.

Hillary Clinton, a high Green and former President Bill Clinton, a very high Orange, may seem quite opposite. But they certainly complement each other very well and contribute in unique ways, and through their own strengths, to their relationship.

Here are two quotes to illustrate their differences: "Clinton means what he says when he says it. But tomorrow he will mean what he says when he says the opposite. He is the existential President, living with absolute sincerity in the passing moment. (from *The New York Times*)

"She loves talking about ideas. But ask her about herself, and she shuts down emotionally" shares a former Wellesley classmate of Hillary Clinton.

In her book *Living History*, Hillary Clinton answers the commonly asked question of how she could possibly stay with her husband. "All I know is that no one understands me better and no one can make me laugh the way Bill does. Even after all these years, he is still the most interesting, energizing and fully alive person I have ever met."

It is very much the desire of both Colors to be challenged and never to be with someone boring – although it shows in much different ways. What was Bill Clinton's first attraction to his future wife? In his words: "She had thick dark blond hair and wore eyeglasses and no makeup, but she conveyed a sense of strength and self-possession I had rarely seen in anyone." Of course, Bill had asked her to get married a number of times very early in their relationship. However Hillary's high Green was, and always will be, her own woman and took quite some time to think over the proposal.

During Clinton's first campaign (for the Arkansas Congress), Hillary quickly took over control of the campaign office. In her words, "there were small wrinkled notes everywhere – typically spilled out onto a desk…(there was an) absolute lack of discipline." Yet the people oriented campaigner and networker, with his incredible skills of motivating people, staying flexible and turning on a crowd are talents that Hillary certainly will never match.

Another example is the very high Gold Nancy Reagan and Orange former President Ronald Reagan. Both contributed greatly to his success as President in ways he would never have been able to do without his Gold wife.

In fact, it is doubtful that he would have ever been elected at all without her focus, attention to detail, drive, management style, stubbornness or ability and willingness to make the hard decisions. After all, Ronald Reagan found it impossible to manage his time well, to say no to a request, or to look at anything other than the positive side of an issue.

Hi George! After the Colors seminar last year, you and I chatted about my boyfriend (high Orange) and me (high Gold/Green). Since that session, our troubles have continued and it has almost come to a parting of ways (as you predicted). Thankfully, we had some good heart-to-hearts and decided we'd rather be happy than be right. As a Gold I was happy to be right, even if it meant he stormed away mad. However, the next day, I'd regret the argument and the reasons for it.

Together we have started to discover small ways to accommodate and appreciate each other's Colors. I have given up some of my 'has-to-be-done-just-so' chores, and it's helped, because now I find with his help, we have more time to spend as a couple enjoying fun stuff – a must have for Oranges, and a reward for hardworking Golds! It's been a challenge as sometimes the dishes aren't where I expect to find them, and there's a bit more dirt than I'd like, but it's a condition that I can live with. It's better than being without him at all.

He, in turn, has left some of the more sensitive/important jobs in my care, understanding that it will bug me to no end if it's not been done to my standards (tax returns, budgeting, paying the bills, cleaning the bathroom). He says he's content to know that he is helping me in some ways, and is pretty thankful that I insist on doing the tedious, detail-oriented tasks that Oranges avoid like the plague!

I appreciate the feedback as it brought perspective to why we were clashing in some of our day-to-day living. My boyfriend and I share a lot of similar interests & passions for life. In understanding each other's Colors, we have a much better chance of going the distance.   — H.M.

Dear H.M.: Oh no, dump that Orange boyfriend. He's actually making you NOT spend your entire life working the to-do list? You having to be flexible and fun, and not take everything so seriously?

'We' didn't decide to be more happy than right – *you* did. Oranges often storm out and forget about things in about an hour. However, these stay on *your* Gold to-do list, and your Green will debrief it for days.

You learned with Colors, and somewhat the hard way that 'lets make a deal' is a really powerful tool – especially with Golds who really prefer to have things done their way. However, what happens with Oranges and Blues is they can often just give up, pretend to be dumb, and let Golds take control... for a while.

Oranges and Blues don't usually want to make an issue out of how to do something – just get 'er done. If Golds step in, Oranges and Blues may step back. The more they step back, the more Golds can take over, and a really vicious cycle begins. Golds can get more resentful over what they started in the first place, but can get in so deep they don't even see it.

Blues Don't Hear So Well

Everyone is familiar with the saying that *actions speak louder than words*. For Blues that is especially true since they live life through their feelings and intuition. But words aren't even one-tenth as powerful as the feeling of being cared about, included, or loved.

In a relationship, you can never tell your Blue partner often enough that you love them or you can never give them too few hugs. When should you tell your partner that you love them? Before someone else does! Many high Greens share that they're just not made that way, and it's just not something they do very frequently. The great news is that we can all grow and learn – quickly!

The feelings of being cared about and loved are infinitely more valuable than words alone. It's the soft touch on the shoulder, the hug, and the eye contact. Feeling loved comes from the energy of holding hands when going for a walk or cuddling on the sofa, and not from words alone.

A recent study actually found that 75% of women and even 73% of men wish their partners would share more often their feelings. Now how hard would that be to implement that with your partner, boyfriend, girlfriend, or spouse? How hard could it be to let your best friend see more of the 'real' you, to grow your relationship in ways you never thought possible.

Your Relationships With Others

The power of Colors also matters in your relationships with in-laws, friends or your co-workers. Here are some brief insights into what other Colors value and look for:

With Orange: Stay active with them and don't slow them down. Be spontaneous, fun and not a drag. Share their optimistic and upbeat conversations and don't ask them to commit to a lot of planning and details. Recognize that they're constantly busy, will not always stay on track and can often change plans and directions.

With Blue: Be receptive to openly share your feelings and thoughts. Praise their creativity and be aware that they wear their heart on their sleeve. Actively listen to them without fixing, as they listen to you, spend quality time one-on-one with them and stay supportive. Blues also value getting together with you rather than communicating by phone or e-mail.

With Green: Be mindful of their need for independence and desire to think things through. Stay aware of their natural curiosity about life and give them things that challenge their problem-solving abilities. Respect their inventions and ideas and remember that they look for credibility and prefer much of their communication by email. This will not be a group that calls you "just to chat," so it'll be up to you to call.

With Gold: Remember to stay on time and on track. Be dependable and loyal and make sure to be extra organized and efficient. Do what you say and return things you borrow promptly. Be aware that they have a close and small circle of friends, a definite line between work and personal life, and a strong sense of privacy. Keep conversations to the point and always call ahead as this group does not want you to just drop by for any reason.